You will go out with joy and be led forth in peace; the

mountains and hills will burst into song before you and

all the trees will clap their hands.

Isaiah 55:12

The joy of the Lord is your strength.

Nehemiah 8:10

I am the light of the world. Whoever follows me will not walk in darkness but will have the light of life.

John 8:12

*He makes me lie down in green pastures.*

*He leads me beside still waters, he restores*

*my soul.* Psalm 23:2-3

Your love, Lord reaches to the heavens, your

faithfulness to the skies.          Psalm 36:5

You rule over the surging sea; when its waves mount up, you still them.          Psalm 89:9

In his hand is the life of every creature

and the breath of all mankind.

Job 12:10

Come to me, all you who are weary and burdened, and I will give you rest.

Matthew 11:28

The Lord gives strength to his people; the

Lord blesses his people with peace.

Psalm 29:11

How countless are your works, Lord! In wisdom you have made them all; the earth is full of your creatures.

Psalm 104:24

Be still and know that I am God.

Psalm 46: 10

Lord, our Lord how majestic is your name in
all the earth.                           Psalm 8:9

Trust in the Lord with all your heart, and

lean not on your own understanding;

In all your ways acknowledge him, and he

shall direct your paths.          Proverbs 3:5

The heavens declare the glory of God, and

the sky above proclaims his handiwork.

Psalm 19:1

For the earth shall be filled with the knowledge of

the glory of the lord, as the waters cover the sea.

Habakkuk 2:14

For I know the plans I have for you declares the lord. Plans to prosper you and not to harm you. Plans to give you hope and a future.

Jeremiah 29:11

The lord himself will go before you. He will be with you. He will not leave you or forget you. Don't be afraid. Don't worry.

Deuteronomy 31:8

He calmed the storm to a whisper and the

waves of the sea were hushed.

Psalm 107:29

He has made everything beautiful in its

time.                    Ecclesiastes 3:11

He is the Maker of heaven and earth, the
sea, and everything in them - he remains
faithful for ever.            Psalm 146:6

The everlasting God is your place of safety. His arms will hold you up forever.　　　Deuteronomy 33:27

The LORD will keep your going out and
your coming in from this time forth and
forevermore.                    Psalm 121:8

Before you created the hills or brought the world into being, you were eternally God and will be God forever.

Psalm 90:2

From the rising of the sun to its setting, the name of the LORD is to be praised!          Psalm 113:3

The deepest places on earth are his. And the highest mountains belong to him.

Psalm 95:4

*All things were made through him, and without him was not anything made that was made.* John 1:3

*God looked over everything he had made; it was*

*so good, so very good!*        Genesis 1:31

Let everything that has breath praise the Lord.

Psalm 150:6

On that day Jesus stood up and said in a loud voice, "If anyone is thirsty, let him come to me and drink. If a person believes in me, rivers of living water will flow out from his heart."     John 7:37

See the birds of the sky, that they don't sow, neither do they reap, nor gather into barns. Your heavenly Father feeds them. Aren't you of more value than they?                                   Matthew 6:26

The lord is my shepherd,

I shall not want.    Psalm 23:1

God is our refuge and strength, a very present

help in trouble.                    Psalm 46:1

Sovereign lord you have made the heavens and the earth by your great power and outstretched arm. Nothing is too hard for you.     Jeremiah 32:17

Shout with joy to the Lord, all the earth.

Burst into songs and praise.  Psalm 98:4

*I can do all things through him who strengthens me.    Philippians 4:13*

*Your righteousness is like the highest mountains*

*your justice like the great deep.*          Psalm 36:6

We know that in everything God works for the good of those who love him. They are the people God called, because that was his plan.

Romans 8:28

*Give all your worries to him because he cares*

*for you.*                                        1 Peter 5:7

Finally be strong in the Lord and in the strength
of his might.                    Ephesians 6:10

Printed in Great Britain
by Amazon

12425985R00045